Table of Contents

Introduction

In a world filled with constant noise, endless distractions, and mounting pressures, finding moments of calm and clarity can seem like an impossible task. Yet, nestled within each of us lies an innate ability to cultivate peace and awareness – a skill that, when nurtured, can transform our lives and the lives of those around us. This transformative power is mindfulness, and it's not just for meditation gurus or enlightened monks. It's a practical, accessible tool that can benefit everyone, from energetic toddlers to stressed-out adults.

"Calm Kids, Cool Adults: Easy Mindfulness for Everyone" is your comprehensive guide to unlocking the potential of mindfulness for yourself and your family. This book demystifies the concept of mindfulness, breaking it down into simple, actionable practices that can be seamlessly integrated into daily life. Whether you're a parent looking to instil valuable coping skills in your children, a teacher seeking to create a more focused classroom environment, or an adult navigating the complexities of modern life, this book offers a roadmap to greater peace, resilience, and joy.

At its core, mindfulness is about paying attention to the present moment without judgement. It's a state of active, open attention to the here and now. While this may sound simple, in practice, it can be challenging to maintain, especially in our fast-paced, technology-driven world. However, the benefits of cultivating this skill are profound and far-reaching. From reduced stress and anxiety to improved focus and emotional regulation, mindfulness has the power to enhance nearly every aspect of our lives.

What sets "Calm Kids, Cool Adults" apart is its holistic, age-inclusive approach to mindfulness. Rather than offering a one-size-fits-all solution, this book recognizes that mindfulness looks different at various stages of life. It provides tailored strategies for children, teenagers, and adults, acknowledging the unique challenges and opportunities that each age group faces. By doing so, it creates a framework for lifelong mindfulness practice that can grow and evolve with you and your family.

One of the key themes explored in this book is the science behind mindfulness. We delve into the fascinating world of neuroscience, exploring how mindfulness practices physically alter our brains, enhancing areas associated with learning, memory, emotional regulation, and empathy. This scientific grounding not only validates the power of mindfulness but also helps readers understand why certain practices are particularly effective. By understanding the 'why' behind mindfulness, you'll be better equipped to embrace and maintain these practices in your daily life.

Another central concept is the idea of creating a mindful haven. In our chaotic world, having a dedicated space and time for mindfulness can make all the difference. We'll guide you through the process of setting up a mindfulness corner in your home, incorporating mindfulness into your daily routines, and selecting age-appropriate tools and resources. This practical approach ensures that mindfulness becomes an integral part of your life, rather than just another item on your to-do list.

For parents and educators, "Calm Kids, Cool Adults" offers a treasure trove of kid-friendly mindfulness techniques. From playful breathing exercises and mindful movement games to gratitude practices and emotional resilience-building activities, you'll find a wealth of engaging ways to introduce mindfulness to young minds. These practices are designed to be fun and accessible, helping children develop crucial life skills while they play and explore.

Teenagers, with their unique set of challenges, receive special attention in this book. We address issues like stress management, self-esteem, body image, and the mindful use of technology. By providing teens with mindfulness tools tailored to their experiences, we aim to empower them to navigate the turbulent waters of adolescence with greater ease and self-awareness.

For adults, the book offers a range of quick, effective mindfulness practices that can be seamlessly integrated into busy schedules. From 5-minute workplace meditations to mindful commuting techniques and desk-friendly stretches, these practices are designed to bring moments of calm and clarity to even the most hectic days. We also explore mindful eating, sleep hygiene, and strategies for managing work-related stress, providing a comprehensive toolkit for adult wellbeing.

"Calm Kids, Cool Adults" is more than just a book – it's an invitation to transform your life through the power of mindfulness. It's a call to slow down, to pay attention, to live more fully in the present moment. It's a roadmap to a life of greater peace, resilience, and joy – not just for you, but for your entire family.

As you turn this page and begin your journey through the book, know that you're taking a significant step towards a more mindful life. The practices and insights you'll encounter in the following chapters have the power to profoundly impact your wellbeing and the wellbeing of those around you. They offer a way to navigate life's challenges with greater ease, to savour life's joys more fully, and to cultivate a deep sense of peace and contentment.

So, take a deep breath, open your mind and heart, and prepare to explore the transformative world of mindfulness. Whether you're a mindfulness novice or a seasoned practitioner, whether you're seeking tools for yourself or for your family, "Calm Kids, Cool Adults" has something valuable to offer. Get ready to discover the calm within the chaos, the clarity within the confusion, and the joy within each present moment. Your mindfulness journey starts now.

…………………..

Chapter 1: Understanding Mindfulness for All Ages

A Simple Guide to Mindfulness

Mindfulness, at its core, is the practice of being fully present and engaged in the current moment. It's about paying attention to our thoughts, feelings, bodily sensations, and surrounding environment without judgement. This simple yet profound concept has gained significant traction in recent years, not just among adults seeking stress relief, but also as a valuable tool for children's emotional and cognitive development.

To truly grasp the essence of mindfulness, consider the words of Jon Kabat-Zinn, a pioneer in bringing mindfulness to mainstream Western culture: "Mindfulness means paying attention in a particular way: on purpose, in the present moment, and non-judgmentally." This definition encapsulates the three key elements of mindfulness: intention, attention, and attitude. When we practise mindfulness, we intentionally direct our attention to the present moment, and we approach our experiences with an open and accepting attitude.

For children, mindfulness can be explained in more concrete terms. It's like using a magnifying glass to look closely at what's happening right now – noticing how their body feels, what thoughts are popping up in their minds, and what's going on around them. It's about being curious about their experiences rather than trying to change them. For instance, a child practising mindfulness might notice the coolness of a breeze on their skin, the sound of birds chirping, or the feeling of excitement bubbling up inside them.

Meanwhile, mindfulness could be how adults remove themselves from the din of their own thoughts and the endless rundowns. This is a moment to take a breather, a moment of stillness in all the busyness. Whether it be savouring the taste of a morning coffee, feeling the sun on their face for however brief a moment during their lunch break or just focusing on breathing for five seconds, mindfulness provides adults with moments of shelter from the relentless pace of modern living.

The Benefits of mindfulness for children and adults

The benefits of mindfulness for both children and adults are numerous and well-documented. For children, mindfulness has been shown to improve attention span, enhance emotional regulation, and boost overall well-being. A study published in the Journal of Child and Family Studies found that mindfulness-based interventions in schools led to significant improvements in students' cognitive performance and resilience to stress.

Children who practise mindfulness often exhibit greater self-awareness and empathy towards others. They become better equipped to handle challenging emotions and situations, leading to improved relationships with peers and family members. Moreover, mindfulness can help children develop a growth mindset, fostering curiosity and openness to new experiences.

For adults, the benefits of mindfulness extend across various aspects of life. Research has consistently shown that regular mindfulness practice can reduce stress, anxiety, and depression. A landmark study published in the Journal of Consulting and Clinical Psychology demonstrated that Mindfulness-Based Stress Reduction (MBSR) was as effective as antidepressant medication in preventing depression relapse.

Beyond mental health, mindfulness has been associated with improved physical health outcomes. It can lower blood pressure, boost immune function, and even slow the progression of age-related cognitive decline. In the workplace, mindfulness has been linked to increased productivity, better decision-making, and enhanced leadership skills.

One of the most significant benefits of mindfulness for both children and adults is its impact on emotional regulation. By practising non-judgmental awareness of their thoughts and feelings, individuals can develop a greater capacity to respond to challenging situations rather than react impulsively. This skill is particularly valuable in today's fast-paced, high-stress world.

Dispelling common myths about mindfulness

Despite the growing body of evidence supporting the benefits of mindfulness, several myths and misconceptions persist. One common myth is that mindfulness is about emptying the mind or achieving a state of constant calm. In reality, mindfulness is not about suppressing thoughts or emotions but rather about observing them without getting caught up in them.

Another misconception is that mindfulness requires long periods of seated meditation. While formal meditation can be a powerful mindfulness practice, it's not the only way to cultivate mindfulness. Brief moments of awareness throughout the day, such as taking a few conscious breaths or paying full attention to a routine task, can be equally beneficial.

For children, there's often a misconception that they lack the attention span or capability to practise mindfulness. However, children are naturally present-minded and curious, making them excellent candidates for mindfulness practice. The key is to present mindfulness in age-appropriate, engaging ways that tap into their natural inclination for play and exploration.

Some adults mistakenly believe that mindfulness is a religious practice or conflicts with their existing beliefs. While mindfulness has roots in Buddhist traditions, modern secular mindfulness is simply a mental training technique that can complement any belief system or worldview. It's about developing awareness and presence, not adhering to any particular spiritual doctrine.

There's also a myth that mindfulness is a quick fix for all of life's problems. While mindfulness can be a powerful tool for managing stress and improving well-being, it's not a panacea. It requires consistent practice and patience to see significant results. As with any skill, the benefits of mindfulness compound over time with regular practice.

One particularly harmful myth is that mindfulness is selfish or self-indulgent. In reality, cultivating mindfulness can lead to greater compassion and empathy towards others. By becoming more aware of our own thoughts and emotions, we become better equipped to understand and respond to the needs of those around us.

For parents and educators, there's sometimes a concern that teaching mindfulness to children might be too complex or abstract. However, numerous child-friendly approaches to mindfulness have been developed, using games, stories, and interactive activities to make the practice engaging and accessible for young minds.

As we dispel these myths, it becomes clear that mindfulness is a versatile and accessible practice that can benefit individuals of all ages. It's not about achieving a particular state of mind, but rather about cultivating a way of being that allows us to engage more fully with our lives.

The beauty of mindfulness lies in its simplicity and universality. Whether you're a child learning to navigate the complexities of social interactions, a teenager grappling with academic pressures and self-identity, or an adult juggling work and family responsibilities, mindfulness offers a way to approach life's challenges with greater clarity and resilience.

As we move forward in exploring the various aspects of mindfulness for different age groups, it's important to remember that mindfulness is a journey, not a destination. It's a skill that can be cultivated and deepened throughout one's lifetime, offering new insights and benefits at every stage of life.

In the next chapter, we'll delve into the fascinating world of neuroscience to understand how mindfulness actually affects our brains. We'll explore the scientific evidence behind the benefits we've discussed and look at how mindfulness practice can lead to measurable changes in brain structure and function across different age groups. This scientific grounding will provide a deeper appreciation for the power of mindfulness and its potential to enhance our lives in profound ways.

. . . .

Chapter 2: The Science of Mindfulness

Neuroscience Meets Mindfulness: Understanding the Connection

As we delve deeper into the world of mindfulness, it's essential to understand the scientific foundation that supports its effectiveness. While the practice of mindfulness has roots in ancient traditions, modern neuroscience has shed light on its profound impact on the brain and overall well-being. This chapter will explore the fascinating intersection of mindfulness and neuroscience, providing insights into how this practice affects our brains and the specific benefits it offers to different age groups.

The human mind is an architectural wonder of intricacy that keeps evolving with every experience it comes across, in synergy with the surroundings. In fact, it is this incredible power to rewire our brains — the core concept of neuroplasticity — that allows mindfulness to change our brain anatomy and function in real time. Take it from **Dr. Richard Davidson**, a groundbreaking neuroscientist in the study of mindfulness — "The brain is continuously being shaped by experience. Nearly all are unaware of the fact that every experience, thought and feeling literally changes our brain. This provides context for how and why mindfulness practice can effect lasting changes to our neural circuitry.

How mindfulness affects the brain

One of the most significant areas of the brain affected by mindfulness is the prefrontal cortex. This region, located just behind the forehead, is responsible for executive functions such as decision-making, planning, and emotional regulation. Studies using functional magnetic resonance imaging **(fMRI)** have shown that regular mindfulness practice can increase the thickness of the prefrontal cortex. This physical change correlates with improved ability to focus, make decisions, and manage emotions effectively. For adults, this can translate into better performance at work and more satisfying personal relationships. In children and adolescents, a strengthened prefrontal cortex can aid in academic performance and social skills development.

The amygdala (that part in the brain also known as "fear centre") is also a key area influenced with mindful practice. The amygdala, an almond-shaped structure in the inside brain, is one of the most important parts of processing emotions—

particularly around fear and stress. Studies show mindfulness practice helps to make the amygdala smaller and less active. In a seminal study published in the journal Biological Psychiatry, after undergoing an eight-week mindfulness-based stress reduction program, participants showed lower stress levels as well as decreased grey matter density in the amygdala. In children and adults, this can translate to higher ability in staying calm under pressure and lower levels of anxiety on a regular basis along with less emotional reactivity.

The hippocampus, a seahorse-shaped structure crucial for learning and memory, also benefits from mindfulness practice. Studies have shown that regular meditation can increase the volume of the hippocampus, potentially enhancing memory formation and recall. This is particularly relevant for older adults, as the hippocampus is one of the first areas of the brain to deteriorate with age and in neurodegenerative diseases like Alzheimer's. For children and teenagers, a well-functioning hippocampus can support better academic performance and the ability to retain new information.

Interestingly, mindfulness practice has been found to affect the default mode network (DMN) of the brain. The DMN is a network of brain regions that are active when we're not focused on the outside world and our mind is wandering. While some mind-wandering can be beneficial for creativity, excessive activity in the DMN is associated with rumination and anxiety. Mindfulness practice has been shown to reduce activity in the DMN, potentially decreasing negative self-talk and promoting a more present-focused state of mind. This effect can be particularly beneficial for adolescents and adults prone to overthinking or excessive worry.

The insula, a region of the brain involved in interoception (the perception of internal bodily sensations) and empathy, also shows increased activity and connectivity with mindfulness practice. This enhanced awareness of bodily sensations can lead to better emotional regulation and increased empathy. For children, this can translate into improved social skills and emotional intelligence. Adults may find that they become more attuned to their own needs and the emotions of others, leading to more fulfilling relationships and improved communication skills.

Age-specific benefits of mindfulness practice

When it comes to age-specific benefits of mindfulness practice, research has uncovered some fascinating insights. In children, mindfulness has been shown to improve attention span, reduce behavioural problems, and enhance overall well-being. A study published in the journal

"Developmental Psychology" found that a school-based mindfulness program led to improvements in cognitive control, working memory, and academic performance in elementary school children. These benefits can set the stage for lifelong learning and emotional resilience.

For teenagers, mindfulness practice can be particularly beneficial during a time of significant brain development and emotional turbulence. The adolescent brain undergoes a period of intense neural pruning and reorganisation, making it especially receptive to the positive effects of mindfulness. Studies have shown that mindfulness can help teenagers manage stress, improve self-esteem, and develop better emotion regulation skills. A notable study published in the "**Journal of Child and Family Studies**" found that a mindfulness program for adolescents led to reduced symptoms of anxiety, depression, and somatic distress.

Adults, too, can reap significant benefits from mindfulness practice. In addition to stress reduction and improved emotional regulation, mindfulness has been shown to enhance cognitive flexibility and creativity in adults. A study published in the journal **"Frontiers in Psychology"** found that even brief mindfulness training could improve divergent thinking, a key component of creativity. For working adults, this can translate into improved problem-solving skills and innovative thinking in the workplace.

Older adults may find mindfulness particularly beneficial for maintaining cognitive function and emotional well-being. Research has shown that mindfulness practice can help slow age-related cognitive decline and may even provide some protection against neurodegenerative diseases. A study published in the journal "Neurobiology of Aging" found that long-term meditators showed less age-related grey matter atrophy compared to non-meditators. Furthermore, mindfulness has been shown to reduce loneliness and improve overall quality of life in older adults.

It's important to note that while the benefits of mindfulness are well-documented, the practice is not a panacea. The effects can vary from person to person, and consistency in practice is key to experiencing long-term benefits. Dr. Sara Lazar, a neuroscientist at Harvard Medical School, emphasises this point: "It's not like you do some mindfulness and then you're done. It's like going to the gym. If you work out once, yes, it's good for you, but you're not going to see big changes. But if you work out regularly, you'll see long-lasting effects."

As we conclude our exploration of the science behind mindfulness, it's clear that this practice has the potential to positively impact individuals across all age groups. From enhancing cognitive function and emotional regulation to reducing stress and improving overall well-being, the neurological benefits of mindfulness are both profound and far-reaching. In the next chapter, we will explore practical ways to create a mindful environment at home, allowing both children and adults to incorporate these brain-boosting practices into their daily lives. By understanding the science and implementing mindfulness techniques, we can nurture calmer kids and cooler adults, creating a more mindful and harmonious world for all.

....

Chapter 3: Cultivate Calm: Creating a Mindful Haven

As we delve deeper into the world of mindfulness, it becomes crucial to understand that our environment plays a significant role in our ability to practise and maintain a mindful state. In this chapter, we'll explore how to create a mindful haven in your home, making it easier for both children and adults to incorporate mindfulness into their daily lives.

Setting up a mindfulness corner at home

Setting up a mindfulness corner at home is an excellent way to designate a specific space for calm and reflection. This area doesn't need to be large; even a small nook can serve as a powerful reminder to pause and breathe. Begin by choosing a quiet spot in your home, away from high-traffic areas and electronic devices. This could be a corner of the living room, a peaceful area in the bedroom, or even a cosy space under the stairs.

Once you've selected the location, consider the elements that will make this space inviting and conducive to mindfulness practice. Soft lighting can create a soothing atmosphere, so consider using a lamp with a warm bulb or string lights for a gentle glow. Comfortable seating is essential – this could be a cushion, a small chair, or even a beanbag for children. The key is to choose something that allows for a relaxed yet alert posture.

Incorporate natural elements to enhance the calming effect of your mindfulness corner. A small plant or a vase of fresh flowers can bring a touch of nature indoors, promoting a sense of peace and connection to the environment. Consider adding a small water feature, such as a tabletop fountain, as the gentle sound of flowing water can be incredibly soothing.

Personalise the space with items that inspire mindfulness and reflection. This could include a favourite quote written on a small chalkboard, a meaningful piece of artwork, or a collection of smooth stones or seashells. For children, include items that engage their senses in a calming way, such as a snow globe, a small zen garden, or a set of worry dolls.

Dr. Jon Kabat-Zinn, a renowned mindfulness expert, emphasises the importance of creating a dedicated space for practice: "Having a special place in your home, even if it's just a cushion in a corner of your bedroom, can help to remind you to practise and can become imbued over time with the energy of your practice."

Incorporating mindfulness into daily routines

Incorporating mindfulness into daily routines is the next step in cultivating a mindful haven. The key is to identify moments throughout the day where you can naturally integrate mindful practices. For adults, this might mean starting the day with a few minutes of meditation before getting out of bed. As you brew your morning coffee or tea, take the opportunity to engage all your senses – notice the aroma, feel the warmth of the mug in your hands, and savour each sip mindfully.

For children, consider establishing a mindful morning routine. This could include taking three deep breaths together before leaving for school or practising a quick body scan to check in with how they're feeling. Bedtime is another excellent opportunity for mindfulness practice. Reading a calming story or engaging in a short guided relaxation can help children transition into a peaceful sleep.

Meal times offer a perfect opportunity for the whole family to practise mindfulness together. Encourage everyone to take a moment of silence before eating to express gratitude for the food. During the meal, practice eating slowly and savouring each bite. This not only promotes mindful eating habits but also creates a sense of connection and presence during family time.

Transitions between activities can be challenging, especially for children. Use these moments as opportunities for brief mindfulness practices. For example, when coming home from school or work, take a few minutes to sit quietly and "shake off" the day before moving on to the next activity. This can help both adults and children transition more smoothly and reduce stress.

Integrating mindfulness into your home environment extends beyond designated practices.

Consider how you can make your entire living space more conducive to calm and awareness. Decluttering can have a significant impact on mental clarity and peace of mind. Work with your family to regularly sort through belongings, keeping only items that are truly needed or bring joy.

Colour psychology can also play a role in creating a mindful haven. Soft, neutral tones like pale blues, greens, and earth tones can promote a sense of calm and relaxation. Consider incorporating these colours into your decor through paint, textiles, or artwork.

The use of natural materials in your home can further enhance a sense of groundedness and connection to nature. Wooden furniture, stone accents, and organic textiles can all contribute to a more mindful living space. Even small touches, like a wooden bowl filled with pinecones or a woven basket for storage, can bring a sense of natural calm to your environment.

Age-appropriate mindfulness tools and resources

Age-appropriate mindfulness tools and resources are essential for making mindfulness accessible and engaging for everyone in the family. For young children, picture books about mindfulness can be a great introduction to the concept. "Breathing Is My Superpower" by Alicia Ortego and "Mindful Monkey, Happy Panda" by Lauren Alderfer are excellent choices that teach mindfulness concepts in a fun, relatable way.

Older children and teens might benefit from mindfulness apps designed specifically for their age group. Apps like Smiling Mind and Headspace for Kids offer guided meditations and activities tailored to different age ranges. These can be particularly helpful for developing a consistent practice and learning various mindfulness techniques.

For adults, there's a wealth of resources available. Books like "Mindfulness: An Eight-Week Plan for Finding Peace in a Frantic World" by Mark Williams and Danny Penman offer structured programs for developing a mindfulness practice. Podcasts such as "Tara Brach" and "10% Happier with Dan Harris" provide regular inspiration and guidance for maintaining mindfulness in daily life.

Physical tools can also enhance your mindfulness practice. A meditation cushion or bench can help maintain proper posture during longer sits. For children, tools like glitter jars or breathing balls can make mindfulness practices more tangible and engaging. A family meditation timer, such as a simple hourglass or a beautifully crafted singing bowl, can be a special object that signifies the beginning and end of practice time.

Remember that creating a mindful haven is an ongoing process. As your family's needs and interests evolve, so too should your mindfulness space and practices. Regularly check in with family members about what's working well and what could be improved. This collaborative approach not only ensures that your mindfulness practices remain relevant and engaging but also reinforces the idea that mindfulness is a shared family value.

As we cultivate calm within our homes, we create a foundation for mindfulness that extends far beyond our four walls. This mindful haven becomes a sanctuary where we can return to our centre, even in the midst of life's chaos. It's a place where children learn to self-regulate, where adults find respite from the demands of daily life, and where families connect in meaningful ways.

In the next chapter, we'll explore specific breathing techniques for kids, building on the foundation of the mindful haven we've created. These fun and engaging exercises will help children develop a greater awareness of their breath, an essential tool for managing emotions and cultivating calm in any

situation.

....

Chapter 4: Breathing Techniques for Kids

As we transition from creating a mindful environment, we now turn our attention to one of the most fundamental aspects of mindfulness practice: breathing. Breathing is the cornerstone of mindfulness, and teaching children to be aware of their breath can have profound effects on their emotional regulation and overall well-being. In this chapter, we will explore fun and engaging breathing exercises designed specifically for children, discuss the use of visual aids to enhance breath awareness, and provide creative ways to incorporate breathing into playtime.

Breathing is a natural process that we often take for granted, yet it holds immense power in calming our minds and bodies. For children, learning to focus on their breath can be a valuable tool for managing emotions, reducing stress, and improving concentration. The key is to make these exercises engaging and enjoyable, turning what might seem like a mundane activity into an exciting adventure.

Fun breathing exercises for children

Let's begin with some fun breathing exercises that children can easily grasp and enjoy. The "Balloon

Breath" is a popular technique that helps children visualise their breath. Instruct the child to imagine their belly is a balloon. As they inhale deeply through their nose, they should picture the balloon inflating, causing their belly to expand. When they exhale slowly through their mouth, the balloon deflates, and their belly contracts. This exercise not only teaches deep breathing but also helps children become aware of the physical sensations associated with breath.

Another entertaining breathing exercise is the "Bumblebee Breath." This technique involves making a gentle humming sound on the exhale, mimicking the buzz of a bee. Have the child take a deep breath in through their nose, and as they exhale, they should close their mouth and make a humming sound. This exercise can be particularly soothing for children who are feeling anxious or overwhelmed, as the vibration created by the humming has a calming effect on the nervous system.

The "Hot Chocolate Breath" is perfect for engaging a child's imagination while teaching controlled breathing. Ask the child to pretend they're holding a mug of hot chocolate. They should breathe in deeply through their nose, as if smelling the delicious aroma. Then, they exhale slowly through their mouth, as if they're cooling down the hot chocolate. This exercise can be especially helpful before bedtime, as it encourages slow, deliberate breathing that can induce relaxation.

For more active children, the "Flower and Candle Breath" can be an excellent choice. Have the child hold one hand out, palm facing up, imagining they're holding a flower. With the other hand, they should hold up an imaginary candle. As they inhale, they should smell the flower deeply, and as they exhale, they blow out the candle gently. This exercise combines imagination with controlled breathing and can be a great way to help energetic children focus and calm down.

Using visual aids to teach breath awareness

Visual aids can significantly enhance a child's understanding and engagement with breathing exercises. One effective tool is a "Breathing Buddy." This can be a small stuffed animal or toy that the child places on their belly while lying down. As they breathe, they watch the toy rise and fall with each breath. This tangible representation of breath movement can help children maintain focus and make the abstract concept of breath more concrete.

Another visual aid that children often enjoy is a "Breathing Sphere" or "Hoberman Sphere." This expandable toy can be opened as the child inhales and closed as they exhale, providing a visual representation of the lungs expanding and contracting. The rhythmic movement of the sphere can be mesmerising for children and helps them pace their breath.

Pinwheels can also serve as excellent visual aids for teaching breath control. Encourage the child to blow on the pinwheel with long, steady breaths to keep it spinning consistently. This not only makes breathing practice fun but also helps children learn to regulate the force and duration of their exhalations.

Incorporating breathing into playtime

Incorporating breathing exercises into playtime can make mindfulness practice feel less like a chore and more like an enjoyable activity. One way to do this is through "Animal Breaths." Encourage children to imitate the breathing patterns of different animals. For example, they can take quick, short breaths like a rabbit, or slow, deep breaths like a sleeping bear. This not only makes breathing practice fun but also helps children understand how different breathing patterns can affect how they feel.

Another playful approach is the "Bubble Breath" game. Provide children with bubble solution and wands, and challenge them to create the biggest bubble they can with one long, steady exhale. This game not only makes breathing practice enjoyable but also helps children learn to control their breath and extend their exhalations.

For a more active breathing game, try "Feather Racing." Place a feather on a flat surface and have children blow it across the room using their breath. This can be turned into a cooperative game where children work together to guide the feather through an obstacle course, or a competitive race to see whose feather reaches the finish line first.

"Breathing Colors" is another creative way to incorporate breathing into playtime. Assign different colours to inhales and exhales. For example, children might imagine breathing in calm blue air and breathing out warm red air. This can be combined with colouring activities, where children use blue crayons while inhaling and red while exhaling, creating a visual representation of their breath.

As we conclude this chapter on breathing techniques for kids, it's important to remember that consistency and patience are key. Not every technique will resonate with every child, so it's beneficial to try various approaches and see what works best. Encourage children to practise these techniques regularly, even when they're feeling calm, so they'll be prepared to use them in moments of stress or excitement.

Breathing exercises can be a powerful tool for children to manage their emotions and find calm in challenging situations. By making these practices fun and engaging, we can help children develop a lifelong habit of mindful breathing. As we move forward to the next chapter on mindful movement for children, we'll explore how combining breath awareness with physical activity can further enhance a child's mindfulness practice, creating a holistic approach to emotional and physical well-being.

. . . .

Chapter 5: Mindful Movement for Children

As we transition from the breathing techniques discussed in the previous chapter, we now explore how mindful movement can further enhance a child's mindfulness practice. Movement is a natural and essential part of a child's life, and by incorporating mindfulness into physical activities, we can help children develop a deeper awareness of their bodies and surroundings.

Simple yoga poses for kids

Simple yoga poses for kids offer an excellent starting point for introducing mindful movement. Child's pose, for instance, is a gentle and comforting position that can help children feel grounded and calm. To guide a child into this pose, have them kneel on the floor, sit back on their heels, and then fold forward, resting their forehead on the ground and stretching their arms out in front of them. Encourage them to focus on their breath and the sensation of their body touching the floor. This pose can be especially helpful for children who feel overwhelmed or anxious, providing a sense of safety and security.

Another accessible yoga pose for children is the tree pose, which helps develop balance and concentration. To practise this pose, have the child stand on one leg and place the sole of the other foot on their inner thigh or calf (never on the knee). Invite them to imagine they are a strong, tall tree with roots growing deep into the ground. This visualisation not only aids in maintaining balance but also fosters a connection with nature. As they hold the pose, encourage them to notice how their body feels and how their breath moves in and out.

The cat-cow pose sequence is an excellent way to introduce children to the concept of linking movement with breath. Starting on hands and knees, guide the child to arch their back and look up towards the ceiling as they inhale (cow pose), and then round their spine and tuck their chin to their chest as they exhale (cat pose). This gentle flow helps children become more aware of their breath and how it can guide their movements.

Mindful walking and running games

While yoga poses provide structured mindful movement, it's also important to incorporate mindfulness into more dynamic activities that children naturally engage in. Mindful walking and running games can transform everyday movements into opportunities for awareness and focus. One such activity is the "Slow Motion Race," where children are challenged to move from one point to another as slowly as possible while staying completely aware of every movement. This game not only cultivates mindfulness but also helps develop patience and body control.

Another engaging mindful walking activity is the "Texture Walk." Take children on a barefoot walk (in a safe, appropriate area) and encourage them to notice the different textures beneath their feet. They might feel the softness of grass, the roughness of concrete, or the coolness of smooth stones. This activity heightened sensory awareness and helps children connect with their environment in a mindful way.

For a more energetic mindful movement game, try the "Freeze Dance." Play music and have children dance freely, but when the music stops, they must freeze in whatever position they're in and hold it until the music resumes. This game not only allows for joyful expression through dance but also cultivates present-moment awareness as children must pay close attention to the music and their bodies.

Incorporating mindfulness into sports and physical education can also be highly beneficial. For instance, before a soccer game or practice, guide children through a brief body scan, helping them notice any tension or excitement in their bodies. This can help them become more attuned to their physical state and emotions, potentially improving their performance and enjoyment of the activity.

Dance and music-based mindfulness activities

Dance and music-based mindfulness activities offer another engaging way to combine movement with awareness. The "Mirror Dance" is a partner activity where one child leads with slow, deliberate movements while the other mirrors them as closely as possible. This exercise requires focus, presence, and body awareness from both participants. It can be done to slow, calming music to enhance the mindful aspect of the activity.

Creating a "Mindful Movement Story" is another creative way to engage children. Tell a story that involves different movements, and have the children act it out. For example, "We're walking through a thick jungle (slow, exaggerated steps), now we're climbing a tall mountain (pretend to climb), and now we're floating down a gentle river (smooth, flowing movements)." This activity combines imagination with mindful movement, making it especially appealing to younger children.

The "Balloon Breath Dance" is a fun way to combine breath awareness with movement. Have children imagine they are balloons, slowly filling up with air as they inhale and stretch their bodies, and then slowly deflating as they exhale and lower back down. This can be repeated several times, with children exploring different ways of "inflating" and "deflating" their balloon bodies.

For a calming, centering activity, try the "Roots and Branches" visualisation. Have children stand with their feet firmly planted on the ground, imagining they have roots growing from their feet deep into the earth. As they inhale, they can raise their arms slowly like branches reaching towards the sky. On the exhale, they can slowly lower their arms. This activity helps children feel grounded and connected to their bodies and the earth.

It's important to remember that mindful movement for children should be playful and engaging. While adults might be content with longer periods of stillness or repetitive movements, children often need variety and creativity to maintain their interest. Don't be afraid to be silly or make animal noises during yoga poses, or to turn mindful walking into a fun exploration game.

Incorporating mindful movement into a child's daily routine can have numerous benefits. It can help improve focus and concentration, reduce stress and anxiety, enhance body awareness and coordination, and foster a sense of calm and well-being. Moreover, by making mindfulness a physical, embodied practice, we make it more accessible and enjoyable for children.

As we conclude this chapter on mindful movement for children, it's worth noting that many of these activities can be adapted for family participation. This not only provides quality bonding time but also allows adults to model mindful behaviour. In the next chapter, we'll explore how to nurture gratitude in children, another essential aspect of mindfulness that can significantly contribute to their overall well-being and happiness.

....

Chapter 6: Raising Thankful Hearts: Nurturing Gratitude in Kids

As we transition from the exploration of mindful movement for children, we now turn our attention to a crucial aspect of mindfulness that can significantly impact a child's emotional well-being and overall outlook on life: gratitude. Chapter 6, aptly titled "Raising Thankful Hearts: Nurturing Gratitude in Kids," delves into the importance of cultivating a sense of appreciation in young minds and provides practical strategies for fostering this essential quality.

Age-appropriate gratitude exercises

Gratitude is more than just saying "thank you" when receiving a gift or a kind gesture. It is a profound appreciation for the positive aspects of life, both big and small. For children, developing a grateful mindset can have far-reaching effects on their emotional development, social relationships, and overall happiness. As parents and caregivers, we have the unique opportunity to shape our children's perspective on the world and help them recognize the abundance that surrounds them.

The concept of gratitude may seem abstract to young children, but with consistent practice and age-appropriate exercises, it can become an integral part of their daily lives. One effective way to introduce gratitude to children is through storytelling. Books that highlight characters expressing thankfulness or overcoming challenges with a positive attitude can serve as powerful tools for initiating conversations about gratitude. For instance, "The Thankful Book" by Todd Parr or "An Awesome Book of Thanks!" by Dallas Clayton can be excellent starting points for discussing the importance of appreciation with younger children.

As children grow older, they can begin to engage in more structured gratitude exercises. A simple yet effective practice is the "Three Good Things" exercise. Each day, preferably before bedtime, encourage your child to reflect on three positive experiences or things they are grateful for. This could be as simple as enjoying a favourite meal, spending time with a friend, or learning something new at school. By focusing on these positive aspects, children begin to train their minds to notice and appreciate the good in their lives, even on challenging days.

For slightly older children, introducing the concept of a gratitude jar can be both fun and impactful.

Place a large, clear jar in a prominent location in your home, along with small slips of paper and pens. Encourage family members to write down moments of gratitude throughout the week and place them in the jar. At the end of each week, gather as a family to read and share these moments. This activity not only reinforces the habit of noticing things to be thankful for but also creates a positive family ritual centred around gratitude.

As children enter their preteen years, they can begin to understand gratitude on a deeper level. Encourage them to think beyond material possessions and consider the people, experiences, and opportunities they are grateful for. This is an excellent time to introduce the practice of writing thank-you notes, not just for gifts received, but for acts of kindness or support from others. Teaching children to express their appreciation in writing helps them articulate their feelings and reinforces the positive impact of gratitude on both the giver and receiver.

Creating gratitude journals with kids

One of the most powerful ways to nurture gratitude in children is through creating and maintaining gratitude journals. This practice can be adapted for various age groups and can evolve as the child grows. For younger children, a gratitude journal might consist of simple drawings or dictated sentences about things they appreciate. As they develop their writing skills, children can begin to write short entries about their daily gratitudes.

When introducing gratitude journaling to children, it's essential to make it an enjoyable and pressure-free activity. Encourage them to decorate their journals and make them personal. Some children might prefer a traditional notebook, while others might enjoy a digital format. The key is to find a method that resonates with the child and encourages consistent practice.

To help children get started with gratitude journaling, provide prompts or questions that spark reflection. For example:

- What made you smile today?
- Who is someone you're thankful to have in your life, and why?
- What's something in nature that you appreciated today?
- What's a skill or ability you're grateful to have?
- What's something you're looking forward to?

As children engage in regular gratitude journaling, they often begin to notice more things to be thankful for in their daily lives. This increased awareness can lead to a more positive outlook and greater resilience in the face of challenges.

Family gratitude rituals

For families looking to incorporate gratitude into their daily routines, establishing family gratitude rituals can be incredibly powerful. These rituals create a shared experience of appreciation and help reinforce the importance of gratitude within the family unit. One simple yet effective ritual is the "gratitude circle" at dinner time. Before or after the meal, each family member takes turns sharing one thing they're grateful for from the day. This practice not only encourages gratitude but also promotes family communication and bonding.

Another family gratitude ritual that can be particularly impactful is the creation of a family gratitude tree or board. This can be a physical display in your home where family members add leaves or notes expressing their gratitudes. As the tree or board fills up over time, it serves as a visual reminder of the many things your family has to be thankful for. This can be especially comforting during challenging times, reminding everyone of the positive aspects of life even when things seem difficult.

For families with older children, consider implementing a monthly or quarterly "gratitude project." This could involve volunteering together at a local charity, creating care packages for those in need, or writing letters of appreciation to community helpers like teachers, firefighters, or healthcare workers. These projects help children develop a sense of perspective and appreciation for their own circumstances while also fostering empathy and a desire to give back to others.

It's important to note that while nurturing gratitude in children is crucial, it should never be forced or used as a way to dismiss their negative emotions. Children, like adults, will experience a range of emotions, and it's essential to validate these feelings. The goal is to help children develop a balanced perspective, where they can acknowledge challenges while still maintaining an overall sense of appreciation for the good in their lives.

As parents and caregivers model gratitude in their own lives, children naturally pick up on this mindset. Be vocal about the things you're grateful for, express appreciation to others in front of your children, and share stories of how gratitude has positively impacted your life. Remember, children are incredibly perceptive and often learn more from what we do than what we say.

In conclusion, nurturing gratitude in children is a lifelong process that requires patience, consistency, and creativity. By incorporating age-appropriate gratitude exercises, creating family rituals, and modelling thankfulness in our own lives, we can help raise children who approach life with a sense of appreciation and wonder. As we move forward to explore mindfulness techniques for teenagers in the

next chapter, we carry with us the understanding
that gratitude forms a crucial foundation for
emotional well-being and resilience at all ages.

....

Chapter 7: Mind Over Mood: Helping Teens Build Emotional Resilience

As adolescents navigate the tumultuous waters of teenage life, they often find themselves grappling with a whirlwind of emotions, social pressures, and academic challenges. The transition from childhood to adulthood can be a particularly stressful period, making it crucial for teens to develop effective coping mechanisms and emotional resilience. Mindfulness offers a powerful toolset for teenagers to manage their emotions, reduce stress, and cultivate a positive self-image. In this chapter, we will explore various techniques and strategies that can help teens harness the power of mindfulness to build emotional resilience and navigate the complexities of adolescence with greater ease and confidence.

Techniques for managing stress and anxiety

Techniques for managing stress and anxiety are essential for teens who often face overwhelming pressures from multiple fronts. One effective approach is the practice of body scanning, which involves systematically focusing attention on different parts of the body, from toes to head, while noting any sensations or tensions. This technique helps teens become more aware of their physical responses to stress and anxiety, allowing them to address these feelings more effectively. For instance, a teen might notice tension in their shoulders during a body scan and consciously relax those muscles, leading to an immediate reduction in stress.

Another powerful technique for stress management is mindful breathing. Encouraging teens to take a few minutes each day to focus on their breath can have profound effects on their emotional well-being. A simple exercise involves counting breaths: inhale for a count of four, hold for a count of four, exhale for a count of four, and hold again for a count of four. This rhythmic breathing pattern, often referred to as "box breathing," can help calm the nervous system and provide a sense of control during stressful situations. As teens become more proficient in this practice, they can use it discreetly in various settings, such as before a challenging exam or during a tense social interaction.

Visualisation is another effective tool for managing stress and anxiety. Teens can be guided to create a mental "safe space" – a calm, peaceful environment they can visualise when feeling overwhelmed. This space could be a real place they've visited or an imaginary location that embodies tranquillity for them. Encourage teens to engage all their senses in this visualisation: what do they see, hear, smell, and feel in their safe space? By regularly practising this visualisation, teens can train their minds to access a state of calm even in the midst of stressful situations.

Mindfulness for self-esteem and body image

Mindfulness for self-esteem and body image is particularly crucial during the teenage years when physical changes and social comparisons can significantly impact a teen's self-perception. One effective approach is to practise self-compassion meditation. This involves guiding teens to direct kind and compassionate thoughts towards themselves, acknowledging their struggles without judgement. For example, a teen might repeat phrases like "May I be kind to myself" or "I accept myself as I am" during meditation. This practice helps counteract the often-harsh self-criticism that many teens experience.

Another powerful technique for building positive self-esteem is the "mirror exercise." Encourage teens to stand in front of a mirror and look at themselves with kindness and acceptance. They can start by focusing on their eyes and gradually expand their gaze to take in their whole appearance. As they do this, they should practise replacing critical thoughts with compassionate ones. For instance, instead of thinking "I hate my acne," they might think "My skin is going through changes, and that's okay." This exercise helps teens develop a more balanced and accepting view of their physical appearance.

To address body image concerns, mindful movement practices can be particularly beneficial. Encourage teens to engage in activities like yoga or dance with a focus on how their body feels rather than how it looks. This shift in perspective can help teens develop a more positive relationship with their bodies, appreciating them for their strength and capabilities rather than just their appearance. As renowned body image researcher Dr. Niva Piran states, "When we connect to our bodies as the vehicles of our lived experience rather than as objects to be evaluated, we develop a more positive embodiment."

Using technology mindfully

Using technology mindfully is increasingly important in today's digital age, where teens are constantly connected to devices and social media. While technology offers many benefits, it can also contribute to stress, anxiety, and negative self-image. Teaching teens to use technology mindfully involves helping them become aware of their digital habits and their impact on their emotional well-being. One effective strategy is to encourage regular "digital detoxes" – periods of time where teens disconnect from their devices and engage in offline activities. This could be as simple as designating meal times as device-free or setting aside one day a week as a "no-phone day."

Another approach to mindful technology use is the practice of "tech check-ins." Encourage teens to pause before reaching for their phones or opening social media apps and ask themselves: "Why am I doing this? How am I feeling right now? How will this action affect my mood?" This simple moment of reflection can help teens become more intentional about their technology use and more aware of its impact on their emotional state.

Social media, in particular, can have a significant impact on teens' self-esteem and emotional well-being. Encourage teens to practise mindful scrolling – being aware of how different posts and interactions make them feel. If they notice that certain accounts or types of content consistently make them feel inadequate or upset, it may be time to reevaluate their social media habits. As psychologist Dr. Sherry Turkle notes, "We need to focus on the quality of our digital connections, not just the quantity."

Teaching teens to set boundaries with technology is also crucial. This might involve turning off notifications during study time or sleep hours, or designating specific times for checking social media rather than constantly being available. By taking control of their digital habits, teens can reduce the stress and anxiety often associated with constant connectivity.

Mindfulness can also be a powerful tool for academic stress management. Many teens experience significant pressure related to school performance and future prospects. Teaching teens to approach their studies mindfully can help reduce this stress and improve their learning outcomes. One effective technique is the Pomodoro method, where teens work intensely for a set period (typically 25 minutes) followed by a short break. During the work periods, teens are encouraged to focus solely on the task at hand, practising present-moment awareness. During the breaks, they can practise quick mindfulness exercises like deep breathing or stretching.

Another helpful approach is mindful goal-setting. Encourage teens to set realistic, specific goals for their academic work, breaking larger tasks into manageable chunks. As they work towards these goals, teens can practise mindful self-reflection, acknowledging their progress without judgement and adjusting their approach as needed. This mindful approach to academic work can help reduce overwhelm and increase a sense of control and accomplishment.

Mindfulness can also be invaluable in helping teens navigate social relationships and peer pressure. Practising mindful communication – really listening to others without judgement and speaking with intention – can improve teens' relationships and reduce social anxiety. Encourage teens to take a moment to check in with themselves before responding in social situations, asking "What am I feeling right now? What do I really want to say?" This pause can help teens respond more authentically and avoid reactive behaviour that they might later regret.

For teens dealing with bullying or social exclusion, mindfulness can provide a source of inner strength and resilience. Loving-kindness meditation, where teens direct wishes of well-being towards themselves and others (including those who may have hurt them), can be particularly powerful in these situations. As mindfulness expert Jon Kabat-Zinn writes, "You can't stop the waves, but you can learn to surf." Mindfulness helps teens develop the emotional skills to "surf" the challenging waves of adolescent social dynamics.

As we conclude this chapter on helping teens build emotional resilience through mindfulness, it's important to remember that developing these skills is a journey, not a destination. Encourage teens to be patient with themselves as they explore these practices, reminding them that mindfulness is called a "practice" for a reason – it takes time and repetition to see its full benefits. By incorporating these mindfulness techniques into their daily lives, teens can develop a robust toolkit for managing stress, building self-esteem, and navigating the challenges of adolescence with greater ease and confidence.

As we move into the next chapter, we'll explore how adults can incorporate quick mindfulness practices into their busy lives, building on the foundation of emotional resilience established in adolescence. Just as teens can benefit from these mindfulness techniques, adults too can find moments of calm and clarity in the midst of their hectic schedules.

....

Chapter 8: Breathe, Relax, Repeat: Quick Mindfulness for Busy Adults

As we transition from discussing mindfulness techniques for teens, we now turn our attention to the busy lives of adults and how they can incorporate mindfulness into their hectic schedules. In this chapter, we'll explore quick and effective mindfulness practices that can be seamlessly integrated into a typical workday.

5-minute mindfulness practices for work

The modern workplace can be a whirlwind of activity, deadlines, and stress. However, even in the busiest of environments, it's possible to find moments of calm and clarity through brief mindfulness exercises. These 5-minute practices can help reset your mind, improve focus, and reduce stress throughout the workday.

One simple yet powerful technique is the "STOP" method. This acronym stands for Stop, take a breath, Observe, and Proceed. When you feel overwhelmed or stressed, pause for a moment. Take a deep breath, focusing on the sensation of air entering and leaving your body. Observe your thoughts, feelings, and physical sensations without judgement. After this brief moment of awareness, proceed with your task with renewed focus and clarity.

Another effective practice is the "body scan." Start by sitting comfortably in your chair, closing your eyes if you feel safe doing so. Begin at the top of your head, bringing your attention to any sensations you feel there. Slowly move your focus down through your face, neck, shoulders, and the rest of your body, noticing any areas of tension or discomfort. As you identify these areas, imagine breathing into them and releasing the tension with each exhale. This practice not only helps you become more aware of your body but also promotes physical relaxation.

For those who find themselves constantly caught up in worry about the future or regret about the past, the "3-3-3" exercise can be a quick way to ground yourself in the present moment. Look around and name three things you can see. Then, identify three sounds you can hear. Finally, move three parts of your body (e.g., your fingers, toes, and shoulders). This simple practice helps redirect your attention to the present, breaking the cycle of rumination and worry.

Mindfulness expert **Jon Kabat-Zinn** once said, "The little things? The little moments? They aren't little." This quote beautifully encapsulates the essence of incorporating brief mindfulness practices into your workday. These small moments of awareness and presence can accumulate, leading to significant improvements in your overall well-being and work performance.

For those who struggle with constant mental chatter or racing thoughts, a brief loving-kindness meditation can be surprisingly effective. Spend a few minutes silently repeating phrases such as "May I be happy, may I be healthy, may I be safe, may I live with ease" to yourself. Then extend these wishes to others – perhaps a coworker, a client, or even someone you're having difficulties with. This practice not only calms the mind but also fosters a sense of connection and compassion in the workplace.

Mindful commuting techniques

For many adults, the daily commute can be a significant source of stress. However, with a shift in perspective, this time can be transformed into an opportunity for mindfulness practice. Whether you're driving, taking public transportation, or walking to work, there are numerous ways to incorporate mindfulness into your commute.

If you're driving, start by taking a few deep breaths before you start the engine. Set an intention to remain present and aware throughout your journey. As you drive, pay attention to the physical sensations of your hands on the steering wheel, your foot on the pedal, and your body in the seat. Notice the colours and shapes of the vehicles around you, the patterns of traffic, and the changing scenery. When you find your mind wandering to work concerns or other stressors, gently bring your attention back to the act of driving.

For those using public transportation, the opportunities for mindfulness are abundant. Instead of automatically reaching for your phone, try spending the first few minutes of your journey in quiet observation. Notice the sounds around you, the feeling of the seat beneath you, the movement of the vehicle. Observe your fellow passengers without judgement, perhaps silently wishing them well. If you choose to read or use your phone, do so mindfully, being fully aware of what you're doing rather than operating on autopilot.

Walking to work offers a perfect opportunity for a moving meditation. Pay attention to the rhythm of your steps, the sensation of your feet touching the ground, and the movement of your arms. Notice the air on your skin, the sounds of the city or nature around you, and the sights along your route. You might choose to coordinate your breath with your steps, perhaps inhaling for four steps and exhaling for four steps.

Renowned meditation teacher Sharon Salzberg notes, "Mindfulness isn't difficult, we just need to remember to do it." This is particularly true when it comes to commuting. By setting an intention to be mindful during your journey to and from work, you can transform what might otherwise be a stressful or tedious part of your day into a valuable opportunity for practice.

For those with longer commutes, you might consider using guided meditations for mindfulness apps. However, be cautious not to become dependent on these tools. The goal is to cultivate your own ability to be present and aware, with or without external guidance.

Desk-friendly stretches and movements

Sitting for long periods at a desk can take a toll on both body and mind. Incorporating mindful movement and stretches into your workday can help alleviate physical tension, increase energy levels, and promote mental clarity. These exercises can be done discreetly at your desk, making them perfect for even the most formal office environments.

Start with a simple neck roll. Drop your chin to your chest and slowly roll your head to the right, back, left, and forward in a circular motion. Do this three times in each direction, paying close attention to any areas of tension or tightness. As you move, focus on your breath, inhaling as you roll back and exhaling as you come forward.

Next, try a seated spinal twist. Sit up straight in your chair, feet flat on the floor. Place your right hand on the outside of your left knee and your left hand behind you on the seat or backrest. Inhale to lengthen your spine, and as you exhale, gently twist to the left, looking over your left shoulder. Hold for a few breaths, then release and repeat on the other side.

For your arms and wrists, which often bear the brunt of keyboard work, try a simple stretch. Extend your arms in front of you, palms facing down. Flex your wrists, pointing your fingers toward the ceiling, then extend them, pointing your fingers toward the floor. Repeat this several times, moving slowly and mindfully.

A discreet way to release tension in your lower back is through a seated cat-cow stretch. Sit at the edge of your chair with your feet flat on the floor. Place your hands on your knees. As you inhale, arch your back and look up slightly (cow pose). As you exhale, round your spine and let your head drop forward (cat pose). Move slowly between these two positions, coordinating your movement with your breath.

Remember, the key to these exercises is not just the movement itself, but the mindful attention you bring to them. As you stretch, notice the sensations in your body. Where do you feel tension? Where do you feel released? How does your breath change as you move?

Yoga teacher and mindfulness advocate **Cyndi Lee** emphasises the importance of bringing awareness to everyday movements: "Mindfulness is simply being aware of what is happening right now without wishing it were different; enjoying the pleasant without holding on when it changes (which it will); being with the unpleasant without fearing it will always be this way (which it won't)."

For those who have the flexibility to do so, consider taking brief "movement breaks" throughout the day. Set a timer to remind yourself to stand up and stretch every hour. Take a short walk around the office or do a few yoga poses in a quiet corner. These breaks not only provide physical benefits but also offer opportunities to reset mentally, potentially boosting productivity and creativity.

As we conclude this chapter on quick mindfulness practices for busy adults, it's important to remember that the goal is not to add another task to your already full plate, but to infuse your existing activities with greater awareness and presence.

In the next chapter, we'll explore how mindfulness can transform our relationship with food, looking at mindful eating practices for both adults and children. We'll discover how bringing awareness to our meals can not only improve our physical health but also enhance our overall enjoyment of life.

....

Chapter 9: Eat, Enjoy, Repeat: Mindful Eating for All Ages

As we transition from discussing mindfulness techniques for busy adults, let's turn our attention to a fundamental aspect of our daily lives that often goes overlooked in our quest for mindfulness: eating. In our fast-paced world, mealtimes can become rushed, distracted affairs, robbing us of the full sensory experience and nutritional benefits that mindful eating can provide. This chapter will explore how we can transform our relationship with food, teaching children healthy habits from an early age, addressing emotional eating in adults, and creating meaningful family mealtime practices.

Teaching children mindful eating habits

Teaching children mindful eating habits is a gift that can last a lifetime. From the moment a child begins to eat solid foods, parents have the opportunity to shape their relationship with food. One effective way to introduce mindful eating to children is through the "rainbow game." Encourage children to notice the different colours on their plate, explaining how each colour represents different nutrients that help their bodies grow strong. Ask them to take a moment before eating to identify all the colours they can see, turning a simple meal into an engaging sensory experience.

Another technique is the "chewing challenge." Many children (and adults) tend to rush through their meals, barely chewing their food. Introduce the idea of counting chews, starting with a goal of chewing each bite 10 times before swallowing. This not only slows down the eating process but also enhances the flavours and textures of the food. As renowned nutritionist and mindful eating expert, Dr. Susan Albers, states, "Mindful eating is not about being perfect, always eating the right things, or never allowing yourself to eat on-the-go again. It's about balance, choice, and experience."

Encouraging children to engage all their senses during mealtimes can make eating a more mindful and enjoyable experience. Before taking a bite, ask them to describe what they see on their plate, what aromas they can smell, and even what sounds they hear as they cut into their food. This multisensory approach not only makes eating more interesting but also helps children develop a deeper appreciation for their food.

It's crucial to remember that children learn by example. If parents and caregivers model mindful eating behaviours, children are more likely to adopt these habits naturally. This means putting away phones and other distractions during mealtimes, eating slowly, and expressing gratitude for the food. Dr. Lilian Cheung, a lecturer at Harvard T.H. Chan School of Public Health, emphasises this point: "Children are natural mindfulness practitioners. They're curious about their food and eager to explore it with all their senses. As adults, we need to nurture this innate mindfulness rather than rush them through meals."

Adult strategies for overcoming emotional eating

As we move from childhood to adulthood, many of us develop complex relationships with food that go beyond simple nourishment. Emotional eating – using food to cope with feelings rather than hunger – is a common challenge that many adults face. Mindful eating can be a powerful tool in overcoming this pattern.

The first step in addressing emotional eating is developing awareness. This involves pausing before eating to check in with yourself. Are you physically hungry, or are you reaching for food because you're stressed, bored, or sad? This simple act of pausing can create a space between the impulse to eat and the action of eating, allowing for more conscious choices.

Dr. Jan Chozen Bays, author of "Mindful Eating: A Guide to Rediscovering a Healthy and Joyful Relationship with Food," suggests using a hunger-fullness scale to gauge physical hunger. On a scale of 1 to 10, with 1 being famished and 10 being uncomfortably full, aim to start eating around 3 or 4 and stop around 6 or 7. This practice helps reconnect with your body's natural hunger and fullness cues, which can often be overridden by emotional eating.

Another strategy for overcoming emotional eating is to develop a "food and mood" journal. For a week or two, write down what you eat, when you eat, and how you're feeling before and after eating. This can help identify patterns and triggers for emotional eating. Once these patterns are recognized, you can work on developing alternative coping strategies for difficult emotions, such as taking a walk, practising deep breathing, or calling a friend.

Mindful eating also involves fully engaging with the eating experience. This means eating without distractions – no TV, no scrolling through your phone, no working at your desk. It means taking the time to appreciate the colours, smells, and textures of your food. It means chewing slowly and savouring each bite. As **Jon Kabat-Zinn**, the founder of Mindfulness-Based Stress Reduction, puts it, "When we taste with attention, even the simplest foods provide a universe of sensory experience."

For many adults, the workplace can be a challenging environment for mindful eating. Rushed lunches at the desk or grazing on snacks during stressful periods are common. To combat this, try implementing a "mindful minute" before eating. Take 60 seconds to sit quietly, breathe deeply, and set an intention for your meal. This brief pause can help transition from work mode to a more present, mindful state for eating.

Family mindful meal practices

Family mealtimes present a unique opportunity to practise mindful eating together and foster stronger connections. In many households, family meals have become less frequent due to busy schedules and competing activities. However, research consistently shows that regular family meals are associated with numerous benefits, including better nutrition, improved academic performance, and reduced risk of substance abuse in adolescents.

To make family meals more mindful, start by creating a calm, pleasant environment. This might involve setting the table nicely, playing soft background music, or lighting a candle. Begin the meal with a moment of gratitude, where each family member shares something they're thankful for. This practice not only cultivates mindfulness but also helps shift the focus from the day's stresses to the present moment.

Encourage conversation during the meal, but steer it away from stressful topics or criticisms. Instead, use this time to share positive experiences from the day or discuss future plans. The goal is to create a warm, supportive atmosphere that everyone looks forward to.

A fun way to incorporate mindfulness into family meals is through "silent meals." Once a week or month, have a meal where no one speaks for the first five minutes. Instead, focus on the sensory experience of eating – the tastes, textures, and aromas of the food. After the silent period, discuss what everyone noticed. This exercise can be eye-opening, revealing how much we often miss when we eat on autopilot.

Another family-friendly mindful eating activity is "mindful food prep." Involve children in meal preparation, teaching them about the ingredients and where they come from. This not only provides valuable life skills but also helps children develop a deeper appreciation for their food. As they help wash vegetables, mix ingredients, or set the table, encourage them to use all their senses and stay present in the task.

For families with younger children, the "tasting game" can be a fun way to introduce mindful eating. Present a variety of foods with different tastes (sweet, sour, salty, bitter) and textures. Blindfold family members and have them guess what they're eating based solely on taste and texture. This game sharpens sensory awareness and can make trying new foods more enjoyable for picky eaters.

It's important to remember that cultivating mindful eating habits is a journey, not a destination. There will be times when we eat mindlessly or use food for emotional comfort, and that's okay. The key is to approach these moments with self-compassion and view them as opportunities for learning and growth.

As we conclude this chapter on mindful eating, it's clear that this practice offers benefits for all ages, from young children just beginning to explore food to adults navigating complex relationships with eating. By bringing greater awareness and intention to our meals, we not only enhance our enjoyment of food but also improve our overall relationship with nourishment and our bodies.

As we move forward to the next chapter, "Mindful Dreams: Sleep Better, Live Better," we'll explore how the mindfulness practices we've discussed can extend into our nighttime routines, improving the quality of our sleep and, by extension, the quality of our waking lives. Just as mindful eating can transform our mealtimes, mindful sleep practices can revolutionise our nights, setting the stage for more peaceful, productive days.

....

Chapter 10: Mindful Dreams: Sleep Better, Live Better

As we transition from exploring mindful eating habits for families, we now turn our attention to another crucial aspect of our daily lives that significantly impacts our overall well-being: sleep. In this chapter, we'll delve into the world of "Mindful Dreams: Sleep Better, Live Better," exploring how mindfulness can transform our sleep experiences and, by extension, our waking lives.

Sleep is a fundamental biological process that plays a vital role in our physical and mental health. Yet, in our fast-paced, technology-driven world, quality sleep often eludes both children and adults alike. The consequences of poor sleep are far-reaching, affecting everything from cognitive function and emotional regulation to physical health and overall life satisfaction. By applying mindfulness principles to our sleep routines, we can cultivate a more restful, rejuvenating sleep experience that sets the stage for more productive, balanced days.

Bedtime routines for children

For children, establishing healthy sleep habits early in life is crucial for their development and well-being. A mindful approach to bedtime routines can help children transition from the excitement of the day to a calm, sleep-ready state. One effective strategy is to create a consistent bedtime ritual that includes gentle, calming activities. This might begin with a warm bath, followed by putting on comfortable pyjamas. The act of changing clothes can serve as a physical signal to the body that it's time to wind down.

Reading a bedtime story is a classic component of many children's bedtime routines, and it can be enhanced with mindfulness principles. Encourage children to fully engage with the story, noticing the details of the illustrations, the sound of your voice as you read, and the feelings the story evokes. This practice of present-moment awareness can help quiet busy minds and prepare children for sleep.

Another powerful tool in a mindful bedtime routine is a body scan meditation. Guide your child to lie comfortably in bed and bring their attention to different parts of their body, starting from their toes and moving up to the top of their head. Encourage them to notice any sensations in each body part without trying to change anything. This practice not only promotes relaxation but also helps children develop body awareness and the ability to self-soothe.

For children who struggle with nighttime anxiety or difficulty falling asleep, introducing a **'worry box'** can be helpful. Before bed, encourage your child to write down or draw any worries or thoughts that are on their mind. These can then be placed in a special box, symbolically setting aside concerns for the night. Explain that the worries will be safe in the box until morning, allowing your child's mind to rest. This practice combines mindfulness with a tangible action, helping to alleviate bedtime stress.

As children grow older, they can take more ownership of their bedtime routines. Encourage tweens and teens to create their own mindful sleep rituals. This might include listening to calming music, practising gentle yoga stretches, or using guided meditation apps designed for young people. By involving them in the process, you're not only promoting better sleep but also teaching valuable self-care skills that will serve them well into adulthood.

Adult sleep hygiene and mindfulness

For adults, the challenges of achieving restful sleep often stem from the inability to "switch off" from the demands of daily life. Mindfulness can be a powerful tool in creating a clear boundary between our waking hours and sleep time. One effective practice is to create a 'mental commute' between work and rest. Just as you might decompress during a physical commute home from work, create a ritual that helps you transition from the active, productive part of your day to a restful state.

This mental commute might involve a short meditation practice, where you consciously review your day, acknowledging accomplishments and letting go of any unfinished tasks or concerns. You might visualise placing your work-related thoughts into a mental briefcase and setting it aside until morning. This practice helps to create a psychological distance from the stresses of the day, allowing your mind to enter a more peaceful state conducive to sleep.

Incorporating mindfulness into your sleep hygiene routine can significantly improve sleep quality. Start by creating a sleep-friendly environment. This means keeping your bedroom cool, dark, and quiet. But beyond these physical aspects, bring mindful awareness to your surroundings. Notice the comfort of your mattress, the softness of your sheets, the weight of your blanket. By fully experiencing these sensations, you're anchoring yourself in the present moment and signalling to your body that it's time to rest.

Dealing with nighttime anxiety and insomnia

Many adults find that racing thoughts or anxiety can prevent them from falling asleep or cause them to wake in the middle of the night. In these moments, mindfulness can be particularly beneficial. Instead of getting frustrated or trying to force sleep, practice accepting your current state of wakefulness. Bring your attention to your breath, noticing the sensation of each inhale and exhale. You might count your breaths or use a mantra like "breathing in calm, breathing out tension" to help focus your mind.

If sleep continues to elude you, instead of tossing and turning, consider practising a lying-down body scan meditation. Start by bringing your awareness to your toes, noticing any sensations present. Gradually move your attention up through your body, consciously relaxing each part as you go. Even if this doesn't lead to sleep, it promotes a state of restful awareness that can be deeply restorative.

For those who struggle with insomnia, mindfulness-based approaches have shown promising results. Mindfulness-Based Therapy for Insomnia (MBTI) combines traditional cognitive behavioural therapy techniques with mindfulness practices. This approach helps individuals develop a different relationship with sleep, reducing the anxiety and effort often associated with trying to fall asleep.

Dr. Jason Ong, a sleep psychologist and researcher at Northwestern University, explains, "Mindfulness helps to reduce the arousal associated with insomnia by teaching people to relate differently to their thoughts and feelings about sleep. Instead of trying to control their sleep, which often backfires, they learn to let go of the struggle with sleep."

One key principle of MBTI is the idea of "falling awake" rather than falling asleep. This subtle shift in perspective can be transformative for those who have developed anxiety around sleep. By bringing gentle, non-judgmental awareness to the experience of lying in bed, without actively trying to sleep, many find that sleep comes more naturally.

Nighttime anxiety is a common issue for both children and adults, often manifesting as racing thoughts, physical restlessness, or a general sense of unease. Mindfulness can be a powerful tool in managing these feelings. One effective technique is the '5-4-3-2-1' grounding exercise. This involves using your senses to anchor yourself in the present moment: identify 5 things you can see, 4 things you can touch, 3 things you can hear, 2 things you can smell, and 1 thing you can taste. This exercise helps to redirect attention away from anxious thoughts and into the present moment.

For those who find themselves waking up in the middle of the night with anxiety, it can be helpful to have a pre-planned mindfulness practice ready. This might be a simple breathing exercise, a short meditation, or even a calming visualisation. The key is to have something familiar and soothing to turn to, rather than getting caught up in anxious thoughts about not being able to fall back asleep.

It's important to note that while mindfulness can be incredibly beneficial for sleep, it's not a quick fix. Like any skill, it requires practice and patience. Encourage both children and adults to approach their sleep mindfulness practice with curiosity and self-compassion. Some nights will be easier than others, and that's perfectly normal.

As we cultivate more mindful sleep habits, we may find that the benefits extend far beyond the nighttime hours. Improved sleep quality can lead to better mood regulation, increased cognitive function, and greater overall well-being. By teaching children mindful sleep practices early on, we're equipping them with valuable tools for lifelong health and resilience.

Moreover, as families adopt mindful sleep practices together, it can create a calmer, more harmonious household atmosphere. The time before bed becomes an opportunity for connection and shared relaxation, rather than a source of stress or conflict.

As we conclude this chapter on mindful dreams, remember that sleep is not just a passive state but an active process of restoration and renewal. By bringing mindfulness to our sleep routines, we're not just improving our nights – we're setting the stage for more vibrant, aware, and fulfilling days.

In the next chapter, we'll explore how mindfulness can enhance our relationships, fostering deeper connections and more harmonious interactions with those around us. We'll discover how the awareness and presence we cultivate in our sleep practices can extend into our waking interactions, creating a ripple effect of mindfulness that touches all aspects of our lives.

. . . .

Chapter 11: The Art of Love & Awareness: Mindfulness for Harmonious Relationships

As we transition from the previous chapter's focus on improving sleep through mindfulness, we now turn our attention to another crucial aspect of our lives: relationships. The quality of our connections with others profoundly impacts our overall well-being and happiness. In this chapter, we'll explore how mindfulness can enhance our relationships, fostering deeper understanding, empathy, and harmony among family members, friends, and colleagues.

Teaching kids empathy and active listening

Teaching kids empathy and active listening is a cornerstone of building mindful relationships from an early age. Children are naturally curious and observant, but they often need guidance to develop a deeper understanding of others' feelings and perspectives. One effective way to nurture empathy in children is through storytelling. Books that feature characters experiencing a range of emotions can serve as excellent conversation starters. After reading, encourage your child to discuss how the characters might have felt and why. This simple exercise helps children practise putting themselves in others' shoes, a crucial component of empathy.

Another powerful tool for teaching empathy is role-playing. Create scenarios where your child can practise responding to others' emotions. For example, you might act out a situation where a friend is feeling sad because they lost a toy. Ask your child how they think the friend feels and what they could do to help. This hands-on approach allows children to explore different emotional responses in a safe, controlled environment.

Active listening is another vital skill that contributes to mindful relationships. For children, learning to listen attentively can be challenging, as their minds are often buzzing with their own thoughts and ideas. One way to practise active listening is through the "repeat back" game. In this activity, one person shares a short story or experience, and the listener must then repeat back the main points they heard. This game not only improves listening skills but also helps children realise how much information they might miss when they're not paying full attention.

For older children and teenagers, introducing the concept of "mindful listening" can be beneficial. Encourage them to focus not just on the words being spoken, but also on the speaker's tone of voice, facial expressions, and body language. This holistic approach to listening helps develop a deeper understanding of the speaker's true message and emotional state.

Mindful communication for adults

As we move from childhood to adulthood, the importance of mindful communication becomes even more apparent. In our fast-paced, technology-driven world, genuine face-to-face communication can sometimes feel like a lost art. Mindful communication for adults involves being fully present in conversations, free from distractions and preconceived notions.

One fundamental aspect of mindful communication is the practice of pausing before responding. This brief moment allows us to process what we've heard, consider our response, and avoid reactive or impulsive remarks that we might later regret. As the Vietnamese Buddhist monk **Thich Nhat Hanh** wisely said, "When you say something that may be difficult for another person to receive, always leave that person with a concrete solution that they can do right away." This approach not only demonstrates empathy but also provides a constructive path forward in potentially challenging conversations.

Another key element of mindful communication is the use of "I" statements. Instead of making accusatory "you" statements, which can put others on the defensive, try expressing your feelings and needs using "I" language. For example, instead of saying, "You never listen to me," you might say, "I feel unheard when I'm speaking and would appreciate your full attention." This subtle shift in language can make a significant difference in how your message is received and can help prevent unnecessary conflicts.

Nonviolent Communication (NVC), a method developed by Marshall Rosenberg, offers a framework for mindful communication that can be particularly useful in conflict resolution. The four components of NVC are observations, feelings, needs, and requests. By focusing on these elements, we can express ourselves clearly and empathetically while also being receptive to others' perspectives.

In intimate relationships, mindful communication takes on even greater importance. Couples who practise mindfulness often report increased relationship satisfaction and better conflict resolution skills. One simple yet powerful mindfulness exercise for couples is the practice of mindful touch. This involves taking a few minutes each day to hold hands or embrace, focusing entirely on the physical sensations and the emotional connection with your partner. This practice can help couples reconnect and ground themselves in the present moment, especially during stressful periods.

Family mindfulness activities for bonding

Family mindfulness activities for bonding provide an excellent opportunity to bring these individual skills together and strengthen relationships within the household. One such activity is the "Gratitude Circle." Gather as a family and take turns expressing gratitude for something each family member has done. This practice not only fosters appreciation but also helps family members feel seen and valued.

Another engaging family mindfulness activity is the "Mindful Meal." For this practice, prepare a meal together as a family, paying close attention to each step of the process. During the meal, eat in silence for the first few minutes, focusing on the tastes, textures, and smells of the food. Then, engage in mindful conversation, perhaps sharing observations about the meal or expressing gratitude for the nourishment. This activity combines mindful eating practices with family bonding, creating a rich, multifaceted experience.

For families with older children or teenagers, a "Digital Detox Day" can be a powerful way to promote mindful interactions. Choose one day a week (or month) where all family members agree to put away their devices and engage in face-to-face activities. This could include playing board games, going for a nature walk, or simply having extended conversations without digital distractions. The absence of screens often leads to more meaningful connections and can help family members rediscover the joy of undivided attention.

Mindfulness can also play a crucial role in navigating the challenges of extended family relationships. Family gatherings, while often joyous, can sometimes be sources of stress or conflict. Practising mindfulness before and during these events can help maintain a sense of calm and perspective. Before a family gathering, take a few minutes to set an intention for how you want to show up in your interactions. During the event, use brief mindfulness techniques, such as taking a few deep breaths or doing a quick body scan, to stay grounded if tensions arise.

In professional relationships, mindfulness can contribute to a more positive and productive work environment. Mindful leadership involves being present and attentive in interactions with colleagues, practising active listening, and responding thoughtfully rather than reacting impulsively. Leaders who embody these qualities often inspire greater trust and respect from their teams.

For employees, practising mindfulness can lead to improved focus, reduced stress, and better relationships with coworkers. Simple practices like taking a few mindful breaths before entering a meeting or practising a brief loving-kindness meditation for colleagues can shift the tone of workplace interactions in a positive direction.

As we cultivate mindfulness in our relationships, it's important to remember that this is an ongoing practice. There will be moments when we fall short, reacting without awareness or failing to listen as attentively as we'd like. The key is to approach these moments with self-compassion and view them as opportunities for growth rather than failures.

Relationship expert John Gottman emphasises the importance of "turning towards" our partners and loved ones, rather than away, in moments of connection. This concept aligns beautifully with mindfulness practices. By being fully present and responsive in our interactions, we create a culture of emotional atonement and support within our relationships.

As we conclude this chapter on mindful relationships, it's clear that the benefits of bringing awareness to our interactions are profound and far-reaching. From teaching children, the foundations of empathy to nurturing deep, meaningful connections in our adult relationships, mindfulness offers a pathway to more harmonious and fulfilling connections with others.

As we move forward to the next chapter, we'll explore how these mindfulness practices can be applied to one of the most pervasive challenges in modern life: stress. By building on the relational skills, we've discussed here, we'll discover how mindfulness can create a buffer against the pressures of daily life, helping both children and adults navigate stressful situations with greater ease and resilience.

....

Chapter 12: Mindfulness for a Stress-Free Life

As we transition from discussing mindful relationships, let's explore how mindfulness can be a powerful tool in managing stress for both children and adults. Chapter 12 focuses on practical techniques for creating a stress-free life through mindfulness, addressing the unique needs of kids, adults, and families.

Kid-friendly stress relief techniques

Kid-friendly stress relief techniques are essential in today's fast-paced world where even children experience significant pressures. One effective approach is the use of visualisation exercises. For instance, children can be guided to imagine a peaceful place, such as a sunny beach or a quiet forest. This mental escape can provide immediate relief from stressful situations. As they picture this serene environment, encourage them to engage all their senses – feeling the warmth of the sun, hearing the gentle waves or rustling leaves, smelling the salt air or pine scent. This multi-sensory approach deepens the relaxation response and makes the experience more vivid and effective.

Another kid-friendly technique is the 'Worry Jar' exercise. Provide children with a physical jar and small pieces of paper. When they feel stressed or worried about something, they can write or draw their concern on a piece of paper and place it in the jar. This act of physically 'containing' their worries can be immensely comforting. It also provides a tangible way for children to externalise their stress, making it seem more manageable. Parents or caregivers can then review the jar with the child at a set time, discussing strategies to address each concern. This not only helps in stress relief but also in developing problem-solving skills.

Body awareness exercises can also be highly effective for children. The 'Body Scan' is a simple yet powerful technique that can be adapted for different age groups. Guide children to lie down comfortably and focus their attention on different parts of their body, starting from their toes and moving up to their head. As they do this, encourage them to notice any areas of tension and imagine breathing into those areas to release the stress. This practice not only helps in immediate stress relief but also teaches children to be more aware of their physical responses to stress in the future.

For slightly older children, introducing the concept of mindful colouring can be beneficial. Colouring intricate patterns or mandalas requires focus and concentration, which naturally pushes away stressful thoughts. The repetitive motion of colouring can induce a meditative state, promoting relaxation. Moreover, the act of creating something beautiful can boost self-esteem and provide a sense of accomplishment, further countering stress.

Music can also be a powerful tool in stress management for kids. Creating a 'Calm Down' playlist with soothing songs or nature sounds can provide children with a go-to resource when they're feeling overwhelmed. Encourage them to listen to this playlist while doing deep breathing exercises or simply lying down and relaxing. The combination of calming sounds and intentional rest can significantly reduce stress levels.

Adult strategies for work-related stress

Transitioning to adult strategies for work-related stress, it's important to recognize that workplace stress is a significant issue for many adults. The American Institute of Stress reports that 83% of US workers suffer from work-related stress, with 25% saying their job is the number one stressor in their lives. These statistics underscore the critical need for effective stress management techniques in the workplace.

One powerful strategy for adults is the practice of mindful breathing at work. This can be as simple as taking a few minutes every hour to focus on your breath. A technique known as '4-7-8 breathing' can be particularly effective. Inhale for a count of 4, hold the breath for a count of 7, and exhale for a count of 8. This pattern activates the parasympathetic nervous system, promoting a state of calm. The beauty of this technique is that it can be done discreetly at your desk, in a meeting, or even while commuting.

Another strategy is the practice of mindful listening. In the workplace, we often find ourselves in conversations or meetings where our minds wander or we're already formulating our response before the other person has finished speaking. Mindful listening involves giving your full attention to the speaker, observing not just their words but also their tone, body language, and the emotions behind their message. This practice not only reduces your own stress by keeping you present but also improves workplace relationships and communication.

For those in high-pressure jobs, the technique of 'micro-mindfulness' can be invaluable. This involves finding small moments throughout the day to practise mindfulness. For instance, you might use the time it takes for your computer to boot up in the morning to do a quick body scan. Or you could use the walk to the water cooler as an opportunity for mindful walking, paying attention to each step and your surroundings. These brief moments of mindfulness can act as reset buttons throughout your workday, preventing stress from accumulating.

Time management is another crucial aspect of reducing work-related stress. The Pomodoro Technique, developed by Francesco Cirillo in the late 1980s, is a time management method that uses a timer to break work into intervals, traditionally 25 minutes in length, separated by short breaks. This technique not only improves productivity but also incorporates regular pauses that can be used for mindfulness practices. During these breaks, you might do some desk stretches, practise deep breathing, or simply close your eyes and let your mind rest for a few moments.

For those dealing with a particularly stressful work environment, it can be helpful to create a 'mindfulness toolkit' for your workspace. This might include items like a small plant (which has been shown to reduce stress and increase productivity), a photograph of a calming scene, a smooth stone to hold during stressful moments, or a journal for quick stress-relieving writing exercises. Having these physical reminders and tools at hand can make it easier to incorporate mindfulness into your workday.

It's also important to address the role of technology in workplace stress. While technology has undoubtedly increased productivity, it has also led to a culture of constant connectivity that can be highly stressful. Practising 'digital mindfulness' involves being intentional about your use of technology. This might mean setting specific times to check emails rather than constantly responding, using apps that block distracting websites during work hours, or even implementing a 'no phone' policy during certain parts of your day. By mindfully managing your relationship with technology, you can significantly reduce work-related stress.

Family approaches to managing household stress

As we shift our focus to family approaches to managing household stress, it's crucial to recognize that stress within the family unit can have a ripple effect, impacting all members. Creating a mindful home environment is key to managing this collective stress. One effective approach is to establish a family mindfulness routine. This could involve a daily 'mindful moment' where the entire family comes together for a brief meditation or gratitude practice. Even just five minutes a day can make a significant difference in reducing overall stress levels and improving family dynamics.

Creating a dedicated 'calm space' in the home can also be beneficial. This could be a corner of the living room or a small nook somewhere in the house, equipped with comfortable seating, some plants, and perhaps a selection of mindfulness tools like books, colouring supplies, or stress balls. Having a physical space associated with calm can provide a refuge for family members when stress levels rise.

Implementing a 'worry time' for the family can also be an effective strategy. Set aside a specific time each day or week where family members can openly discuss their concerns or stresses. This not only provides a structured outlet for expressing worries but also prevents stress from constantly infiltrating family time. During these sessions, practise active listening and validate each other's feelings. Follow up by brainstorming solutions together, teaching problem-solving skills while also showing that the family is a team in tackling challenges.

Mindful communication is another crucial aspect of managing household stress. Encourage family members to practise 'I' statements when expressing feelings or concerns. For example, instead of saying "You always leave your stuff everywhere," one might say "I feel frustrated when I see belongings scattered around." This approach reduces defensiveness and opens up more constructive dialogue. Also, introduce the concept of a 'pause button' in heated moments. When tensions rise, any family member can call for a brief pause to take a few deep breaths before continuing the conversation.

Physical activity can be a great way to manage stress as a family. Engaging in mindful movement together not only reduces stress but also strengthens family bonds. This could be as simple as a family yoga session, a mindful nature walks, or even a dance party in the living room. The key is to approach these activities with full presence and awareness, encouraging everyone to focus on their breath and bodily sensations as they move.

Mindful meal times can also play a significant role in reducing household stress. In many families, meals can become rushed affairs or sources of conflict. By approaching meals mindfully, you can transform them into opportunities for connection and relaxation. This might involve having everyone help in meal preparation, setting the table beautifully, expressing gratitude before eating, and focusing on the sensory experience of the food.

Encourage conversation during meals, but try to steer clear of stressful topics, making mealtime a peaceful respite in the day.

It's also important to address the impact of external stressors on the family unit. News and social media, for instance, can be significant sources of stress. Consider implementing a 'media-free' time in your household, where all devices are turned off and the family engages in screen-free activities together. This not only reduces exposure to potentially stressful information but also creates space for more meaningful interactions.

Lastly, remember that managing household stress is an ongoing process that requires flexibility and patience. What works for your family may change over time, and that's okay. The key is to approach stress management with a spirit of openness, compassion, and teamwork. By working together to create a mindful home environment, families can not only reduce stress but also build stronger, more resilient relationships.

As we conclude this chapter on mindfulness for a stress-free life, it's clear that stress management is a multifaceted endeavour that requires different approaches for children, adults, and families. By incorporating these mindfulness techniques into daily life, it's possible to create a more peaceful, balanced existence. In the next chapter, we'll explore how mindfulness can be integrated into educational settings, enhancing the learning experience for both students and teachers.

....

Chapter 13: Learning with Awareness: Mindfulness in the Educational Journey

As we transition from discussing mindfulness in family and home settings, it's essential to explore how these practices can be integrated into the educational environment. The classroom, a place where children spend a significant portion of their time, presents unique opportunities and challenges for implementing mindfulness techniques. This chapter delves into the various ways mindfulness can be incorporated into the educational journey, benefiting students, teachers, and the overall learning experience.

Classroom mindfulness activities

Classroom mindfulness activities form the cornerstone of bringing awareness practices into schools. These activities can be seamlessly woven into the fabric of daily routines, creating moments of calm and focus amidst the often-chaotic school day. One effective approach is to start each class with a brief mindfulness exercise. This could be as simple as a one-minute breathing exercise where students are encouraged to close their eyes, focus on their breath, and let go of any distracting thoughts. This short practice can help students transition from one subject to another, or from recess back to the classroom, allowing them to settle and refocus their attention.

Another valuable classroom activity is the "mindful listening" exercise. In this practice, the teacher rings a bell or plays a calming sound, and students are asked to raise their hand when they can no longer hear the sound. This not only sharpens auditory awareness but also teaches children to pay attention to the present moment. As renowned mindfulness expert Jon Kabat-Zinn notes, "The little things? The little moments? They aren't little." These seemingly small exercises can have a profound impact on a child's ability to concentrate and engage with their learning environment.

For older students, incorporating mindful journaling can be particularly beneficial. At the beginning or end of each day, students can be given a few minutes to write about their thoughts, feelings, or experiences. This practice not only enhances self-awareness but also improves writing skills and emotional expression. Teachers can provide prompts related to the day's lessons or more general mindfulness themes, encouraging students to reflect on their learning process and personal growth.

Movement-based mindfulness activities can also be incredibly effective, especially for younger children who may struggle with sitting still for extended periods. Simple yoga poses or stretching exercises can be integrated into the school day, perhaps during transitions between subjects or as a brief break during longer classes. These physical practices not only promote mindfulness but also help to release tension and increase blood flow, which can enhance cognitive function and overall well-being.

Mindfulness for improved focus and learning

Mindfulness for improved focus and learning is another crucial aspect of bringing awareness into the educational setting. The ability to concentrate is fundamental to the learning process, yet in today's world of constant stimulation and digital distractions, many students struggle to maintain focus. Mindfulness practices can significantly enhance a student's capacity for sustained attention and cognitive flexibility.

One effective technique for improving focus is the "anchor" practice. Students are taught to choose an anchor – typically the breath, but it could also be a physical sensation or a specific point in the room – and continually return their attention to this anchor whenever they notice their mind wandering. This simple yet powerful practice trains the brain to recognize distractions and consciously redirect focus, a skill that is invaluable in both academic and real-world settings.

Another approach to enhancing focus through mindfulness is the practice of "noting." In this technique, students are encouraged to mentally label their experiences as they arise – for example, "thinking," "hearing," or "feeling." This helps to create a small gap between the experience and the reaction to it, allowing students to observe their thoughts and sensations without becoming overly caught up in them. As they develop this skill, students become better able to manage distractions and maintain concentration on their studies.

Mindfulness can also be integrated into specific subject areas to enhance learning. For instance, in a science class studying ecosystems, students might be guided through a mindful observation of a natural object, such as a leaf or a rock. By paying close attention to the object's details – its texture, colour, shape – students not only practise mindfulness but also develop their observational skills, which are crucial in scientific inquiry.

In literature classes, mindful reading practices can deepen students' engagement with texts. By encouraging students to read slowly and attentively, noticing their reactions and the images that arise in their minds, teachers can foster a more immersive and meaningful reading experience. This approach can lead to richer discussions and more insightful analyses of literary works.

Mathematics, often considered a challenging subject for many students, can also benefit from mindfulness practices. By teaching students to approach maths problems with a calm and focused mind, free from anxiety and self-doubt, teachers can help reduce maths anxiety and improve problem-solving skills. Simple breathing exercises before tests or challenging lessons can help students enter a more relaxed and receptive state of mind.

While the benefits of mindfulness for students are clear, it's equally important to consider teacher self-care and mindfulness practices. Educators face numerous stressors in their daily work, from managing classroom behaviour to meeting academic targets and dealing with administrative demands. Mindfulness can provide teachers with valuable tools for managing these challenges and maintaining their own well-being.

One essential practice for teachers is to start and end each day with a brief mindfulness exercise. This could involve a few minutes of deep breathing, a body scan, or a short meditation. By bookending the school day with these moments of calm, teachers can create a buffer between their personal and professional lives, helping to reduce stress and increase resilience.

Teacher self-care and mindfulness practices

Throughout the day, teachers can benefit from incorporating micro-moments of mindfulness into their routines. For example, taking three conscious breaths before responding to a challenging student behaviour can help maintain composure and respond more effectively. Similarly, practising mindful walking while moving between classrooms or during playground duty can provide brief moments of centering and renewal.

Mindfulness can also enhance teachers' ability to be present and responsive in the classroom. By cultivating moment-to-moment awareness, educators can become more attuned to their students' needs and the overall classroom dynamics. This heightened awareness can lead to more effective teaching strategies and a more positive learning environment.

Moreover, mindfulness practices can help teachers develop greater emotional regulation, which is crucial in managing the often-intense emotions that can arise in educational settings. As mindfulness expert Daniel Siegel points out, "Mindfulness lets you be aware of your mental state so you can regulate it more effectively." By learning to observe their thoughts and emotions without immediately reacting to them, teachers can respond to challenging situations with greater calm and wisdom.

Incorporating mindfulness into staff meetings and professional development sessions can also be beneficial. Starting meetings with a brief mindfulness practice can help participants transition into a more focused and receptive state of mind. Additionally, offering mindfulness training as part of ongoing professional development can provide teachers with valuable tools for managing stress and enhancing their overall well-being.

It's important to recognize that implementing mindfulness in educational settings is not without its challenges. Some students or staff members may be sceptical or resistant to these practices. It's crucial to introduce mindfulness in a way that is secular, evidence-based, and respectful of diverse backgrounds and beliefs. Emphasising the practical benefits of mindfulness, such as improved focus and reduced stress, can help overcome initial resistance.

Another challenge is finding time for mindfulness practices in an already packed school day. However, as we've seen, many mindfulness activities can be brief and easily integrated into existing routines. The key is to start small and gradually build a culture of mindfulness within the school community.

As we look to the future of education, mindfulness has the potential to play an increasingly important role. In a world where information is readily available at our fingertips, the ability to focus, reflect, and engage deeply with learning becomes even more crucial. By integrating mindfulness into the educational journey, we can help students develop not just academic knowledge, but also essential life skills that will serve them well beyond their school years.

As we conclude this chapter on mindfulness in education, it's clear that these practices have the power to transform the learning experience for both students and teachers. By creating more aware, focused, and emotionally balanced educational environments, we lay the foundation for deeper learning and greater well-being. In the next chapter, we'll explore how mindfulness can be extended beyond the classroom and into the natural world, examining the profound connections between mindfulness and our relationship with nature.

....

Chapter 14: Green Space, Calm Mind: Mindfulness in Nature

As we transition from exploring mindfulness in educational settings, we now turn our attention to the profound connection between mindfulness and nature. The natural world offers a unique and powerful backdrop for cultivating awareness, presence, and inner calm. In this chapter, we'll delve into the myriad ways both children and adults can harness the restorative power of nature to enhance their mindfulness practice.

Outdoor mindfulness activities for kids

Children are natural explorers, and the outdoors provides an endless playground for their curiosity and imagination. By introducing mindfulness practices in natural settings, we can help children develop a deeper connection with the world around them while fostering a sense of calm and awareness.

One effective way to engage children in outdoor mindfulness is through sensory exploration. Encourage kids to use all their senses to experience nature fully. For example, have them close their eyes and listen intently to the sounds around them – the rustling of leaves, the chirping of birds, or the babbling of a nearby stream. Ask them to describe what they hear, helping them focus their attention on the present moment.

Another engaging activity is the "nature treasure hunt." Instead of searching for specific items, encourage children to find objects that appeal to their senses. They might look for something soft, rough, colourful, or fragrant. This activity not only sharpens their observational skills but also helps them practise mindful attention to detail.

Walking meditation can be adapted for children in natural settings. Guide them to walk slowly and deliberately, paying attention to the sensation of their feet touching the ground. Encourage them to notice how different surfaces feel – the softness of grass, the crunch of gravel, or the firmness of a wooden path. This practice helps children develop body awareness and grounding techniques.

For more active children, a "mindful movement" game can be both fun and entertaining. Instruct them to move like different animals they might encounter in nature – slithering like a snake, hopping like a frog, or soaring like an eagle. As they imitate these movements, ask them to pay attention to how their bodies feel and how their movements change based on the animal they're mimicking.

Creating nature mandalas is another excellent way to combine creativity with mindfulness. Invite children to collect natural materials like leaves, pebbles, and flowers, and arrange them in circular patterns. This activity encourages focus, patience, and appreciation for the beauty and impermanence of nature.

Renowned child psychologist Dr. Maria Montessori once said, "There is no description, no image in any book that is capable of replacing the sight of real trees, and all the life to be found around them, in a real forest." This quote beautifully encapsulates the importance of direct nature experiences for children's development and well-being.

Adult practices for connecting with nature

For adults, nature offers a respite from the constant stimuli of modern life and provides an ideal setting for deepening mindfulness practice. The natural world invites us to slow down, breathe deeply, and reconnect with our innate sense of wonder and presence.

One powerful practice for adults is "forest bathing," a concept originating from Japan known as "Shinrin-yoku." This practice involves immersing oneself in the atmosphere of the forest, engaging all senses to absorb the natural environment. To practise forest bathing, find a wooded area and walk slowly, allowing your attention to be drawn to whatever catches your senses – the play of sunlight through leaves, the texture of tree bark, or the earthy scent of the forest floor.

Research has shown that forest bathing can reduce stress hormone production, lower heart rate and blood pressure, boost the immune system, and improve overall well-being. Dr. Qing Li, author of "Forest Bathing: How Trees Can Help You Find Health and Happiness," explains, "The key to unlocking the power of the forest is in the five senses. Let nature enter through your ears, eyes, nose, mouth, hands and feet."

Mindful gardening is another excellent way for adults to connect with nature while practising mindfulness. Whether tending to a small window box or a large vegetable garden, the act of nurturing plants can be deeply meditative. Pay attention to the feel of soil in your hands, the subtle changes in your plants from day to day, and the rhythmic nature of watering and weeding. Gardening teaches patience, presence, and the acceptance of things beyond our control – all vital aspects of mindfulness.

For those living in urban environments, finding green spaces might require more effort, but it's no less important. City parks, rooftop gardens, or even a single tree on a busy street can serve as focal points for nature-based mindfulness. Practise mindful breathing while sitting on a park bench, or take a few moments to really observe a flower growing through a crack in the sidewalk. These small connections with nature can provide powerful moments of presence and calm amidst the urban bustle.

Water-based mindfulness practices can be particularly soothing for adults. If you have access to a beach, lake, or river, spend time sitting quietly by the water's edge. Focus on the rhythmic sound of waves or the flowing current. Watch how light plays on the water's surface. This practice can induce a meditative state and foster a sense of connection with the larger natural world.

Stargazing is a profound way to practise mindfulness while connecting with nature on a cosmic scale. On a clear night, find a dark spot away from city lights. Lie back and gaze at the vast expanse of the night sky. Allow yourself to be filled with a sense of wonder at the immensity of the universe. This practice can help put daily worries into perspective and foster a sense of interconnectedness with all of existence.

Family nature-based mindfulness experiences

Engaging in nature-based mindfulness as a family can strengthen bonds, create lasting memories, and instil a lifelong appreciation for both mindfulness and the natural world. These shared experiences provide opportunities for open communication, mutual support, and collective growth.

One simple yet powerful family activity is a "gratitude nature walk." As you stroll through a park or forest, take turns sharing things in nature for which you're grateful. This might be as grand as a beautiful sunset or as small as an interesting pebble. This practice combines the benefits of physical activity, nature connection, and gratitude – all key components of well-being.

Creating a family "sit spot" ritual can be a wonderful way to regularly connect with nature and each other. Choose a special outdoor location – perhaps a favourite tree in your backyard or a quiet corner of a nearby park. Visit this spot regularly as a family, sitting quietly and observing how the area changes with the seasons. This practice fosters a sense of place and helps family members tune into the subtle rhythms of the natural world.

Nature journaling as a family activity can blend mindfulness, creativity, and environmental education. Provide each family member with a notebook and encourage them to record their observations, thoughts, and feelings about their natural experiences. This might include sketches of plants or animals, descriptions of weather patterns, or reflections on how being in nature makes them feel. Sharing these journals can lead to rich family discussions and a deeper appreciation for each person's unique perspective.

Mindful photography can be an engaging way for families to practise presence in nature. Instead of quickly snapping photos, encourage family members to really look at their surroundings before taking a picture. What caught their attention? What emotions does the scene evoke? This practice can help develop a more contemplative approach to both nature and technology.

For families with older children or teens, participating in conservation activities can be a meaningful way to practise mindfulness while giving back to nature. Whether it's planting trees, cleaning up a beach, or maintaining hiking trails, these activities foster a sense of stewardship and connection to the environment. They also provide opportunities to practise mindfulness through physical work and focused attention.

Nighttime nature experiences can be particularly magical for families. Organise a family moonlight walk, paying attention to how familiar surroundings look different in the soft lunar light. Or have a backyard campout, practising mindful listening to nighttime sounds and stargazing together. These experiences can create a sense of adventure and wonder while providing unique opportunities for mindfulness practice.

As we conclude this exploration of mindfulness in nature, it's clear that the natural world offers a rich tapestry of opportunities for cultivating awareness, calm, and connection. Whether through solo practices, family activities, or community engagement, nature-based mindfulness can profoundly enhance our well-being and our relationship with the world around us. As we move forward, we'll explore how to sustain these practices and integrate them into a lifelong journey of mindfulness and growth.

. . . .

Chapter 15: Sustaining a Lifelong Mindfulness Practice

As we conclude our journey through the various aspects of mindfulness for children and adults, it's crucial to address the challenge of sustaining a lifelong mindfulness practice. This final chapter will explore how to create lasting habits, overcome common obstacles, and continue growing in your mindfulness journey.

Creating personal and family mindfulness routines

Creating personal and family mindfulness routines is essential for maintaining a consistent practice. For adults, this might mean setting aside time each morning for meditation or mindful breathing exercises. Dr. Jon Kabat-Zinn, founder of Mindfulness-Based Stress Reduction (MBSR), emphasises the importance of consistency: "The best way to capture moments is to pay attention. This is how we cultivate mindfulness. Mindfulness means being awake. It means knowing what you are doing." With this in mind, consider integrating mindfulness into your daily activities, such as brushing your teeth mindfully or taking a few deep breaths before checking your phone in the morning.

For families, establishing a shared mindfulness routine can be both bonding and beneficial. This could involve a weekly family meditation session, where everyone gathers in a comfortable space to practise together. Start with short sessions, perhaps just five minutes, and gradually increase the duration as everyone becomes more comfortable. Another approach is to incorporate mindfulness into existing family rituals. For example, before dinner, you could have a moment of silence where everyone reflects on their day and expresses gratitude for the meal.

Children thrive on routine, so consistency is key when introducing mindfulness practices. A bedtime mindfulness ritual can be particularly effective. This might involve guiding your child through a brief body scan or a calming visualisation exercise. As they grow older, encourage them to lead these sessions themselves, fostering independence in their mindfulness practice.

It's important to remember that mindfulness routines should be flexible and adaptable. Life is unpredictable, and rigid adherence to a specific schedule can sometimes create more stress than it alleviates. Instead, focus on creating a general framework that can be adjusted as needed. This might mean having a "mindfulness menu" of different practices that family members can choose from based on their mood and energy levels on any given day.

Overcoming common obstacles to regular practice

As you work to establish these routines, it's natural to encounter obstacles. One of the most common challenges is finding time for mindfulness in our busy lives. Many people feel that they simply don't have the space in their schedules for "one more thing." However, as mindfulness teacher Sharon Salzberg points out, "Mindfulness isn't difficult, we just need to remember to do it." The key is to start small and integrate mindfulness into existing activities rather than trying to carve out large chunks of time.

For example, you might practise mindful walking during your commute, paying close attention to each step and the sensations in your body. Or, you could use the time spent waiting in line at the grocery store as an opportunity for a quick breathing exercise. By finding these small pockets of time throughout the day, you can cultivate mindfulness without significantly altering your schedule.

Another common obstacle is the misconception that mindfulness practice should always feel peaceful or relaxing. In reality, mindfulness is about being present with whatever arises, whether it's pleasant or unpleasant. There may be days when your mind feels particularly busy or when sitting still seems impossible. It's crucial to approach these experiences with curiosity and non-judgment, rather than seeing them as failures.

Thich Nhat Hanh, the renowned Buddhist teacher, offers this perspective: "The present moment is filled with joy and happiness. If you are attentive, you will see it." This reminder can be particularly helpful on days when mindfulness feels challenging. By shifting your focus to the simple act of being present, rather than trying to achieve a particular state of mind, you can overcome the obstacle of unrealistic expectations.

For children, boredom or restlessness can be significant barriers to maintaining a mindfulness practice. To address this, it's important to keep sessions short and engaging. Incorporate elements of play and creativity into mindfulness activities. For instance, you might use a snow globe as a visual aid for a calming exercise, asking the child to watch the swirling glitter settle as they focus on their breath. Or, you could create a "mindfulness treasure hunt," encouraging children to use their senses to notice different objects or sensations in their environment.

As adults, we often face the challenge of self-judgement and perfectionism in our mindfulness practice. We might berate ourselves for having a wandering mind or feel frustrated when we miss a day of meditation. It's crucial to approach these moments with self-compassion. As psychologist and mindfulness expert Kristin Neff reminds us, "With self-compassion, we give ourselves the same kindness and care we'd give to a good friend."

When you notice yourself being self-critical about your mindfulness practice, try to pause and acknowledge these thoughts with gentleness. Remind yourself that mindfulness is a lifelong journey, not a destination. Every moment is an opportunity to begin again, regardless of how long it's been since your last formal practice.

Technology can be both a help and a hindrance in sustaining a mindfulness practice. On one hand, there are numerous apps and online resources available to support your journey. These can be particularly helpful for beginners or those looking to expand their practice. However, the constant connectivity and distractions of our digital world can also make it challenging to stay present and focused.

To navigate this, consider setting boundaries around technology use. This might involve designating certain times of day as "device-free" or using apps that limit screen time. At the same time, explore how technology can support your mindfulness practice. Many meditation apps offer guided sessions and reminders to help you stay on track. The key is to use technology mindfully, as a tool to enhance your practice rather than a source of distraction.

Resources for continued learning and growth

As you continue on your mindfulness journey, it's important to seek out resources for continued learning and growth. This might involve reading books on mindfulness, attending workshops or retreats, or joining a local mindfulness group. Engaging with a community of like-minded individuals can provide support, accountability, and new perspectives on your practice.

For families, look for resources that cater to different age groups and interests. There are many children's books that introduce mindfulness concepts in accessible ways, as well as family-friendly mindfulness programs and classes. Encourage older children and teens to explore their own mindfulness interests, whether that's through apps, podcasts, or joining youth mindfulness groups.

Remember that the path of mindfulness is not linear. There will be periods of intense engagement and growth, as well as times when your practice feels stagnant or challenging. This is all part of the journey. As **Jon Kabat-Zinn** says, **"You can't stop the waves, but you can learn to surf."** By approaching your practice with curiosity, compassion, and a willingness to begin again, you can navigate the ebbs and flows of a lifelong mindfulness journey.

In conclusion, sustaining a lifelong mindfulness practice is about finding balance, consistency, and adaptability. By creating personal and family routines, overcoming common obstacles, and continually seeking out new resources and experiences, you can cultivate a rich and rewarding mindfulness practice that evolves with you over time. Remember that every breath, every moment of awareness, is an opportunity to deepen your connection with yourself and the world around you. As you move forward from this book, carry with you the tools and insights you've gained, and trust in your innate capacity for mindfulness and growth.

....

Conclusion

Throughout this book, we've explored the transformative power of mindfulness for people of all ages. From breathing techniques for kids to stress management for busy adults, we've seen how simple awareness practices can cultivate calm, boost emotional resilience, and enhance overall well-being. The science is clear: mindfulness changes our brains and our lives for the better.

We've discovered that mindfulness isn't just about sitting in silence. It's a versatile tool that can be integrated into every aspect of life - from eating and sleeping to learning and communicating. By bringing awareness to our daily activities, we can find more joy in the present moment and build stronger, more harmonious relationships with ourselves and others.

For children, mindfulness offers a foundation for emotional intelligence and self-regulation. It equips them with valuable tools to navigate the challenges of growing up in today's fast-paced world. For adults, it provides a much-needed respite from stress and a path to greater clarity and purpose. Together, families can use mindfulness to create stronger bonds and a more peaceful home environment.

The journey of mindfulness is lifelong, and each person's path is unique. By establishing regular practices and overcoming common obstacles, we can sustain our mindfulness journey through all of life's ups and downs. Remember, every moment is an opportunity to be mindful. With patience, persistence, and compassion for ourselves, we can cultivate a more aware, calm, and fulfilled existence.

As you close this book, consider the small steps you can take today to bring more mindfulness into your life and the lives of those around you. The practices shared here are not meant to be perfect - they're meant to be lived. Embrace the journey with an open heart and a curious mind. In doing so, you'll discover that true calm isn't found in perfect stillness, but in meeting each moment with awareness and grace.

....